Felix Mendelssohn Bartholdy

A Midsummer Night's Dream
Ein Sommernachtstraum

5 Orchestral Pieces
Op. 61

Edited by / Herausgegeben von
Boris von Haken

EULENBURG

EAS 161
ISBN 978-3-7957-6561-3
ISMN 979-0-2002-2549-5

Ernst Eulenburg Ltd
48 Great Marlborough Street
London W1F 7BB

Contents / Inhalt

Preface

Composed: 1826/1843 in Berlin
First performance: 14 October 1843 in Potsdam, conducted by the composer
Original publisher: Breitkopf & Härtel, Leipzig
Instrumentation: 2 Flutes, 2 Oboes, 2 Clarinets, 2 Bassoons – 2 Horns,
3 Trumpets, 3 Trombones, Tuba, Ophicleïde – Timpani, Cymbals – Strings
Duration: ca. 30 minutes

When Mendelssohn moved to Berlin in July 1841 at the invitation of King Friedrich Wilhelm IV of Prussia, it was with the idea of reforming Protestant church music in the city, but in the event this was a challenge that he was either unable or unwilling to confront, with the result that in October 1842, following an audience with the king, Mendelssohn wrote to ask for his permission to return to Leipzig as director of the Gewandhaus concerts. In doing so, Mendelssohn forwent half his salary, while declaring that once he was back in Leipzig he would 'carry out all the tasks that Your Majesty deigns to entrust to me and do so, moreover, with the greatest love and to the best of my abilities'.[1] Among these tasks was that of providing incidental music for the Royal Court Theatre in Berlin. In a letter to Karl Klingemann of 23 November 1842 we find Mendelssohn announcing that there were a number of pieces that he had to write 'at the special request of the king'.[2] One of these requests was for incidental music for a new production of Shakespeare's *A Midsummer Night's Dream*, a commission first mentioned in this letter to Klingemann. By 17 January 1843 we find Mendelssohn again writing to Klingemann, informing him that he has now started work on the score. In spite of this, it is not possible to reconstruct the compositional process in every detail. The first night of the new production of the work – the first to be staged in Germany – was finally set for 14 October 1843, the day before the king's birthday. The work was performed in the translation of August Wilhelm Schlegel and directed by Ludwig Tieck, who had been appointed dramaturge at the Royal Court Theatre at Berlin in 1841. Ludwig Devrient, who took the part of Lysander, reports that the rehearsals began in the Elisabeth Hall of the Royal Palace in Berlin on 27 September as the huge sets that had to be built for the production prevented the theatre from operating normally:[3] part of the action was to be staged on a reconstruction of an

[1] Letter from Mendelssohn to Friedrich Wilhelm IV, 28 October 1842, quoted in Paul and Carl Mendelssohn Bartholdy, ed. *Briefe aus den Jahren 1830 bis 1847 von Felix Mendelssohn Bartholdy* (Leipzig, 1870), 487.
[2] Letter from Mendelssohn to Karl Klingemann, 23 November 1842, quoted in Mendelssohn Bartholdy, *Briefe aus den Jahren 1830 bis 1847* (note 1), 489–90.
[3] Eduard Devrient, 'Meine Erinnerungen an Felix Mendelssohn-Bartholdy und seine Briefe an mich', *Dramatische und Dramaturgische Schriften*, 10 vols. (Leipzig, 1869), Vol. X, 238–41

VI

Elizabethan theatre. Although Mendelssohn was back in Berlin with the finished score by mid-September, it was not until 5 October that he and the orchestra were invited to attend the stage rehearsals, when an unforeseen problem immediately arose. Tieck had run together the second, third and fourth acts of the play, believing that the resultant three-act structure most closely approximated to the ideal of classical unity. Mendelssohn, by contrast, had written his music with Shakespeare's five-act original in mind. As a result, the two entr'actes – the Intermezzo No. 5 and the Notturno No. 7 – were now superfluous, at least from a dramaturgical standpoint. But the overall musical design of the music evidently made it impossible for Mendelssohn simply to cut these two numbers, and so they were performed with the curtains open. In order to justify this course of events, Tieck had the figure of Hermia – or Hermina, as she is called in Schlegel's translation – silently act out the line 'Either death or you I'll find immediately' while looking for Lysander. Meanwhile the orchestra played the Intermezzo. The entrance of the Rude Mechanicals was likewise accompanied by music. According to Fanny Hensel, they were to express 'by means of comic gestures their pleasure at the beauties of nature'.[4] For the transition between the third and fourth acts, Lysander, Demetrius, Helena and Hermia lay asleep on the ground to the strains of the Notturno. But the 'protracted sight of the sleeping couples was simply embarrassing', according to Eduard Devrient, and so Tieck attempted to salvage the scene by having 'set pieces representing bushes pushed in front of the lovers in order to hide them', an expedient which in Devrient's view created a 'coarsely theatrical impression that at the same time was in dubious taste'.[5] It was presumably during these rehearsals that Mendelssohn made an important change to the score, adding cymbals to the Wedding March, having earlier decided to do without them.[6]

The first night on 14 October 1843 was a private performance at the Court Theatre at the Neues Palais in Potsdam, the king's summer residence. The first public performance took place four days later at the Royal Court Theatre in the capital. According to the composer's early biographer August Reissmann, the music was 'performed with such precision, and the dynamic resources that Mendelssohn employed here were used with a consciousness that had hitherto scarcely been thought possible in an orchestra'.[7]

For subsequent performances, Mendelssohn prevailed on the Gewandhaus Orchestra bassoon player, Louis Weißenborn, to prepare a copy of his score,[8] but it was not until four years later that he decided to publish the work. He wrote to his publisher on 25 October 1847: 'I finally think it may be time to bring out the music for the Midsummer Night's Dream in

[4] Letter from Fanny Hensel to Rebekka Mendelssohn, 18 October 1843, quoted in Sebastian Hensel, ed., *Die Familie Mendelssohn*, 2 vols. (Leipzig, 1924), Vol. II, 263–7
[5] Devrient, 'Meine Erinnerungen an Felix Mendelssohn-Bartholdy' (note 3), 239
[6] On this point, see Ferdinand David's letter to Mendelssohn, quoted in Julius Eckardt, *Ferdinand David und die Familie Mendelssohn* (Leipzig, 1888), 188–9.
[7] August Reissmann, *Felix Mendelssohn-Bartholdy: Sein Leben und seine Werke*, third edition (Leipzig, 1893), 288
[8] Letter from Mendelssohn to Louis Weißenborn, 2 December 1843, quoted in *Leipziger Ausgabe der Werke von Felix Mendelssohn Bartholdy*, Series V: Stage Works, Vol. VIII: *Musik zu Ein Sommernachtstraum*, op. 61, ed. Christian Martin Schmidt (Wiesbaden, Leipzig and Paris, 2000), XV

full score and orchestral parts. If you agree, I would preface the work with a short introduction with regard to concert performances and send this to you in due course after I have looked through the proofs.'[9] By this date, however, Mendelssohn's health was already seriously impaired. Three days later he suffered a stroke and died on 4 November 1847. The full score of *A Midsummer Night's Dream* was finally published after his death without any further involvement on his part.

Boris von Haken
Translation: Stewart Spencer

---

[9] Letter from Mendelssohn to Breitkopf & Härtel, 25 October 1847, Staatsbibliothek zu Berlin, shelfmark Härtel no. 30, quoted by Schmidt, *Musik zu Ein Sommernachtstraum* (note 8), XVII

Vorwort

komponiert: 1826/1843 in Berlin
Uraufführung: 14. Oktober 1843 in Potsdam unter der Leitung
des Komponisten
Originalverlag: Breitkopf & Härtel, Leipzig
Orchesterbesetzung: 2 Flöten, 2 Oboen, 2 Klarinetten, 2 Fagotte – 2 Hörner,
3 Trompeten, 3 Posaunen, Ophikleide – Pauken, Becken – Streicher
Spieldauer: etwa 30 Minuten

Seit Juli 1841 lebte Felix Mendelssohn in Berlin, wohin ihn der Preußische König Friedrich Wilhelm IV. berufen hatte. Seine ursprüngliche Aufgabe, die gesamte evangelische Kirchenmusik zu reformieren, konnte oder wollte Mendelssohn nicht erfüllen. Bereits im Oktober 1842, nach einer Audienz beim Monarchen, bat er schriftlich um die Erlaubnis, nach Leipzig zurückkehren zu dürfen, wo er wieder die Leitung der Gewandhaus-Konzerte übernehmen wollte. Mendelssohn verzichtete dabei auf die Hälfte seines Gehalts und erklärte, er werde die „Aufträge, welche mir Ew. Majestät zu geben geruhten, [...] dort mit der größten Liebe und mit meinen besten Kräften ausführen"[1]. Hierzu gehörte auch die Komposition von Bühnenmusiken für das Königliche Schauspielhaus. In einem Brief an Karl Klingemann vom 23. November 1842 berichtet Mendelssohn, er habe „einzelne Arbeiten im besonderen Auftrag des Königs zu machen"[2]. Dazu gehört auch die Musik zu Shakespeares *Ein Sommernachtstraum*, die an dieser Stelle erstmals erwähnt wird. Am 17. Januar 1843 schreibt Mendelssohn an Klingemann, er habe nun mit der Arbeit begonnen. Der Verlauf des Kompositionsprozesses ist jedoch nicht im Detail zu rekonstruieren. Die Premiere wurde schließlich auf den 14. Oktober 1843, einen Tag vor dem Geburtstag von Friedrich Wilhelm IV. festgelegt. Die Inszenierung dieser Erstaufführung von Shakespeares *Sommernachtstraum* in der Übersetzung von August Wilhelm Schlegel übernahm Ludwig Tieck, der das Amt eines Dramaturgen des Königlichen Schauspiels ausübte. Ludwig Devrient, der die Rolle des Lysander spielte, berichtet, dass die Proben am 27. September im Elisabethen-Saal des königlichen Schlosses in Berlin begannen, da das Aufstellen des großdimensionierten Bühnenbilds den regulären Theaterbetrieb des Schauspielhauses behindert hätte.[3] Tieck hatte für einen Teil der Handlung einen Nachbau des Londoner Shakespeare-Theaters vor-

---

[1] Brief Mendelsssohns an Friedrich Wilhelm IV., 28. Oktober 1842, in: Paul Mendelssohn Bartholdy/Carl Mendelssohn Bartholdy (Hg.), *Briefe aus den Jahren 1830 bis 1847 von Felix Mendelssohn Bartholdy*, Leipzig 1870, S. 487.
[2] Brief Mendelssohns an Karl Klingemann, 23. November 1842, in: ebd. S. 489–490.
[3] Devrient, Eduard: *Meine Erinnerungen an Felix Mendelssohn-Bartholdy und seine Briefe an mich* (Dramatische und Dramaturgische Schriften, Bd. 10), Leipzig 1869, S. 238–241.

gesehen. Mendelssohn, der aus Leipzig mit der fertigen Partitur angereist war, wurde mit dem Orchester erst am 5. Oktober zu den Bühnenproben hinzugezogen. Dabei entstanden jedoch ungeahnte Schwierigkeiten. Ludwig Tieck hatte den zweiten, dritten und vierten Akt der Komödie zu einem einzigen großen Akt zusammengefasst, da er sich mit dieser, nun dreiteiligen Disposition dem Ideal einer klassischen Geschlossenheit annähern wollte. Dagegen war Mendelssohn nach der Vorlage Shakespeares von fünf Akten ausgegangen. Damit waren jedoch die Zwischenaktmusiken, das Intermezzo Nr. 5 und das Notturno Nr. 7, zumindest dramaturgisch überflüssig geworden. Die musikalische Gesamtdisposition Mendelssohns ließ es jedoch offenkundig nicht zu, auf diese beiden Musikstücke zu verzichten. Sie mussten nun bei geöffnetem Vorhang gespielt werden. Um den Ablauf dennoch szenisch zu rechtfertigen, ließ Tieck die Figur der Hermina die Suche nach Lysander im Anschluss an die letzte Textzeile „Entweder den Tod oder dich will ich finden auf der Stelle" („Either death or you I'll find immediately") pantomimisch darstellen, während dazu nun das Intermezzo gespielt wurde. Auch der folgende Auftritt der sechs Rüpel musste zur Musik erfolgen. Nach dem Bericht von Fanny Hensel sollten sie durch „lustige Gebärden ihr Wohlgefallen an der schönen Natur" zum Ausdruck bringen.[4] Bei dem Übergang vom dritten zum vierten Akt lagen Lysander, Demetrius, Helena und Hermina zum Notturno schlafend auf der Bühne. Da dieser „langdauernde Anblick der schlafenden Liebespaare peinlich" wirkte, ließ Tieck zur Rettung der Szene „Versetzstücke von Buschwerk zur Deckung der Liebenden" vorschieben, was nach der Ansicht Eduard Devrients jedoch „plump theatralisch und bedenklich dazu"[5] wirkte. Vermutlich noch während der Proben hat Mendelssohn noch eine wichtige Ergänzung an seiner Partitur vorgenommen. Der Instrumentation des Hochzeitsmarsches fügte er Becken hinzu, auf die er ursprünglich verzichtet hatte.[6]

Die Uraufführung am 14. Oktober 1843 war eine geschlossene Vorstellung im Schlosstheater des Neuen Palais in Potsdam, der Sommerresidenz von Friedrich Wilhelm IV. Die erste öffentliche Aufführung folgte am 18. Oktober im Königlichen Schauspielhaus. August Reissmann schreibt über die musikalische Gestaltung, dass „eine solche Präcision der Aufführung, eine so bewusste Anwendung der dynamischen Mittel, wie sie hier Mendelssohn erreicht hatte, […] bisher im Orchester kaum für möglich gehalten" wurde[7].

Für weitere Aufführungen lässt Mendelssohn durch Louis Weisenborn, Fagottist des Gewandhausorchesters in Leipzig, eine Kopie seiner Partitur erstellen.[8] Erst vier Jahre später entscheidet er sich, das Werk im Druck zu veröffentlichen. Am 25. Oktober 1847 schreibt er an seinen Verleger: „Endlich würde ich glauben, daß es vielleicht an der Zeit sei, die Musik zum Sommernachtstraum in Partitur und Orchesterstimmen erscheinen zu lassen. Wenn Sie

---

[4] Brief von Fanny Hensel an Rebekka Mendelssohn, 18. Oktober 1843, in: Sebastian Hensel (Hg.), *Die Familie Mendelssohn*, Leipzig 1924, Bd. 2, S. 263–267.

[5] Devrient, Eduard, a. a. O.

[6] Vgl. zu dieser Ergänzung den Brief Ferdinand Davids an Mendelssohn in: Julius Eckardt, *Ferdinand David und die Familie Mendelssohn*, Leipzig 1888, S. 188–189.

[7] Reissmann, August: *Felix Mendelssohn-Bartholdy. Sein Leben und seine Werke*, Leipzig 1893, S. 288.

[8] Schreiben Mendelssohns an Louis Weisenborn, 2. Dezember 1843, zitiert in: *Leipziger Ausgabe der Werke von Felix Mendelssohn Bartholdy*, Serie V, Bühnenwerke, Bd. 8: *Musik zu Ein Sommernachtstraum*, op. 61, Christian Martin Schmidt (Hg.), Wiesbaden/Leipzig/Paris 2000, S XV.

dieser Meinung sind, so würde ich eine Vorbemerkung hinsichtlich der Concert-Aufführungen dem Werke vordrucken lassen, und Ihnen seiner Zeit nach Durchsicht der Correkturen zu schicken".[9] Zu diesem Zeitpunkt ist jedoch die Gesundheit Mendelssohns bereits ernsthaft bedroht; drei Tage später erleidet er einen Schlaganfall und stirbt am 4. November 1847. Die Partitur der Musik zum *Sommernachtstraum* wird schließlich posthum ohne die Mitwirkung Mendelssohns publiziert.

Boris von Haken

---

[9] Brief Mendelssohns an Breitkopf & Härtel, 25. Oktober 1847, Staatsbibliothek zu Berlin, Slg. Härtel Nr. 30; zitiert nach Schmidt, a. a. O. S. XVII.

A Midsummer Night's Dream
5 Orchestral Pieces

Felix Mendelssohn Bartholdy
(1809–1847)
Op. 61

I. Scherzo
Allegro vivace

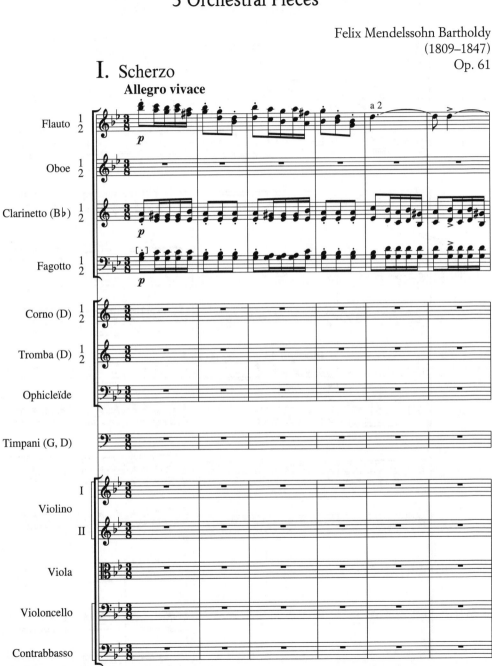

EAS 161

Edited by Boris von Haken
© 2009 Ernst Eulenburg Ltd, London
and Ernst Eulenburg & Co GmbH, Mainz

4

6

9

12

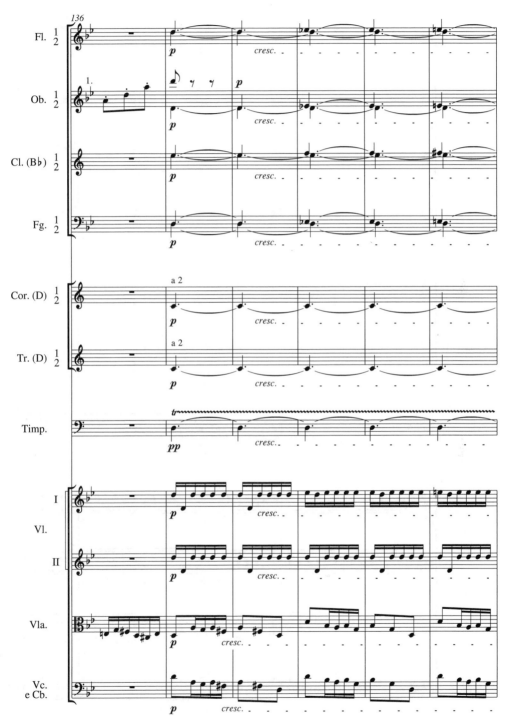

16

18

20

22

24

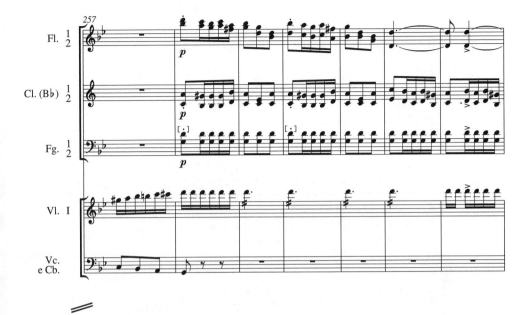

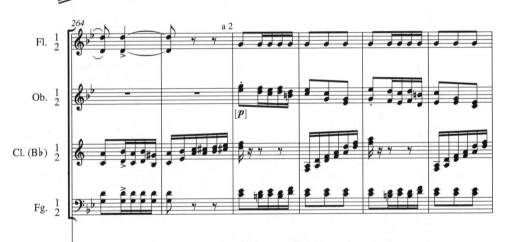

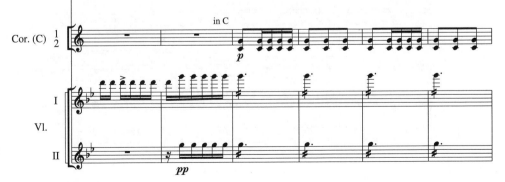

II. Intermezzo

Allegro appassionato

44

48

52

54

60

III. Notturno

Andante tranquillo

IV. Hochzeitsmarsch/Wedding March

Op.61/9

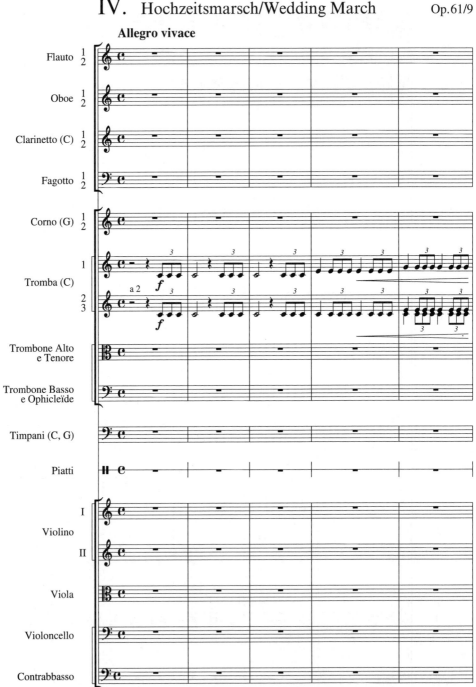

80

EAS 161

86

EAS 161

EAS 161

V. Ein Tanz von Rüpeln/Bergomask

Op.61/11

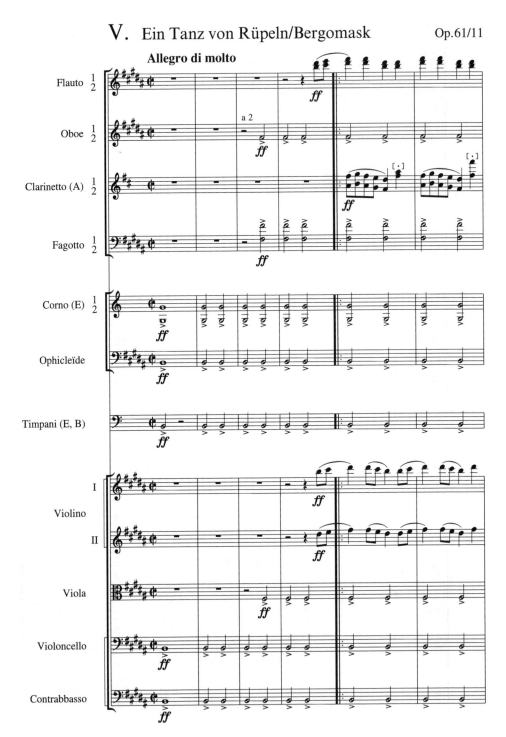